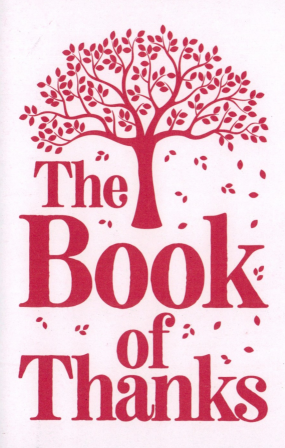

Published 2024
FiNGERPRINT!
An imprint of Prakash Books India Pvt. Ltd

113/A, Darya Ganj,
New Delhi-110 002
Email: info@prakashbooks.com/sales@prakashbooks.com

📘 Fingerprint Publishing
❎ @FingerprintP
📷 @fingerprintpublishingbooks
www.fingerprintpublishing.com

ISBN: 978 93 5856 844 8

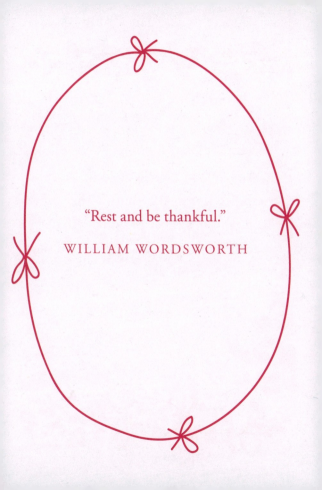

"Rest and be thankful."

WILLIAM WORDSWORTH

"At times, our own light goes out and is rekindled by a spark from another person. Each of us has cause to think with deep gratitude of those who have lighted the flame within us."

ALBERT SCHWEITZER

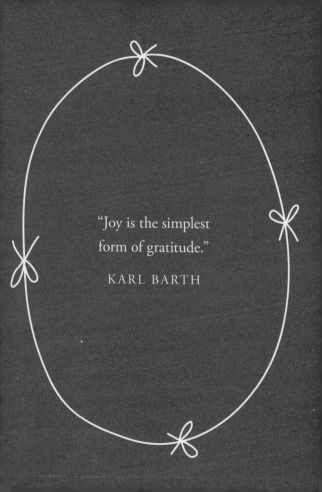

"Joy is the simplest form of gratitude."

KARL BARTH

"The deepest craving
of human nature is the
need to be appreciated."

WILLIAM JAMES

"Now is no time to think
of what you do not have.
Think of what you can
do with what there is."

ERNEST HEMINGWAY

"Being thankful is not always experienced as a natural state of existence, we must work at it, akin to a type of strength training for the heart."

LARISSA GOMEZ

"Opening your eyes to more of the world around you can deeply enhance your gratitude practice."

DERRICK CARPENTER

"Gratitude is the sweetest fragrance that fills your heart when you count your blessings, even when they are disguised as challenges."

ANONYMOUS

"Be thankful for what you have;
you'll end up having more.
If you concentrate on what
you don't have, you will never,
ever have enough."

OPRAH WINFREY

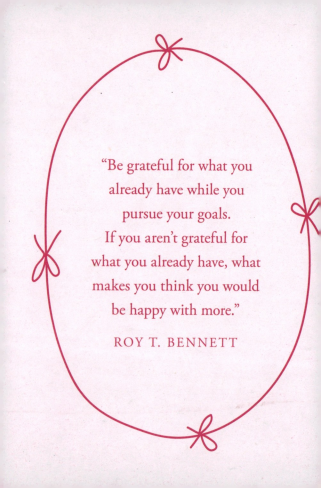

"Be grateful for what you already have while you pursue your goals. If you aren't grateful for what you already have, what makes you think you would be happy with more."

ROY T. BENNETT

"As with all commandments, gratitude is a description of a successful mode of living. The thankful heart opens our eyes to a multitude of blessings that continually surround us."

JAMES E. FAUST

"We often take for granted
the very things that most
deserve our gratitude."

CYNTHIA OZICK

HOW TO CULTIVATE THE ATTITUDE OF GRATITUDE?

* Keep a gratitude journal and take a few minutes each day to write down three things you are grateful for.

* Whether it's through a sincere compliment, or simply saying "thank you" in person, acknowledge the support of others to strengthen relationships.

* Throughout the day, whenever something brings you joy or appreciation, write it down in the 'Notes' app of your phone. At the end of the week or month, take time to read through these moments.

* Show gratitude by sharing specific examples of how someone's actions or words have positively impacted your life.

"If you concentrate on finding
whatever is good in every situation,
you will discover that your life will
suddenly be filled with gratitude,
a feeling that nurtures the soul."

RABBI HAROLD KUSHNER

"The unthankful heart discovers no mercies; but let the thankful heart sweep through the day and, as the magnet finds the iron, so it will find, in every hour, some heavenly blessings."

HENRY WARD BEECHER

"Gratitude is the attitude that sets the altitude for living."

ANONYMOUS

"Make it a habit to tell people, 'thank you.' To express your appreciation sincerely and without the expectation of anything in return. Truly appreciate those around you, and you'll soon find many others around you. Truly appreciate life, and you'll find that you have more of it."

RALPH MARSTON

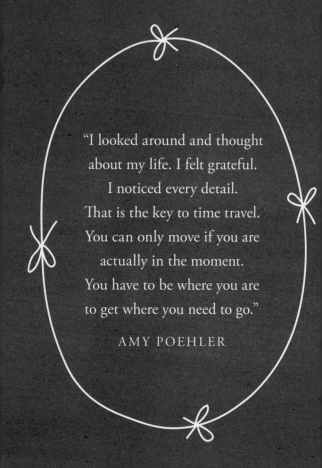

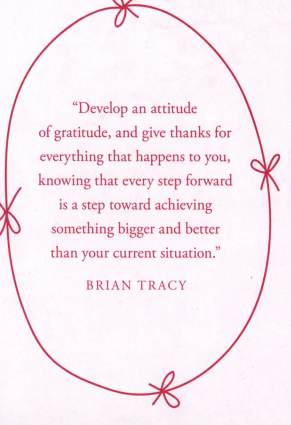

"Develop an attitude of gratitude, and give thanks for everything that happens to you, knowing that every step forward is a step toward achieving something bigger and better than your current situation."

BRIAN TRACY

"Train yourself never to put off the word or action for the expression of gratitude."

ALBERT SCHWEITZER

"One can never pay in gratitude;
one can only pay
'in kind' somewhere
else in life."

ANNE MORROW LINDBERGH

"Gratitude, like faith,
is a muscle.
The more you use it,
the stronger it grows."

ALAN COHEN

"The world has enough beautiful mountains and meadows, spectacular skies and serene lakes. It has enough lush forests, flowered fields and sandy beaches. It has plenty of stars and the promise of a new sunrise and sunset every day. What the world needs more of is people to appreciate and enjoy it."

MICHAEL JOSEPHSON

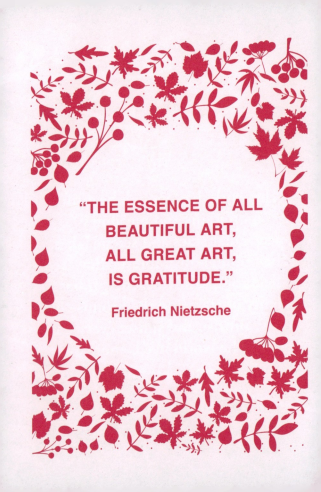

"I cried because I had no shoes, then I met a man who had no feet."

MAHATMA GANDHI

"We can always find something to be thankful for, and there may be reasons why we ought to be thankful for even those dispensations which appear dark and frowning."

ALBERT BARNES

"There is a calmness to a life
lived in gratitude, a quiet joy."

RALPH BLUM

"I don't have to chase extraordinary moments to find happiness—it's right in front of me if I'm paying attention and practicing gratitude."

BRENÉ BROWN

"Gratitude for the present moment and the fullness of life now is the true prosperity."

ECKHART TOLLE

"A grateful mind is a great mind which eventually attracts to itself great things."

PLATO

"I've found in my life that the easiest way to increase my joy is to religiously practice gratitude until I'm a gratitude machine!"

RHONDA BYRNE

"Gratitude turns what we have into enough."

ANONYMOUS

"No one who achieves success does so without the help of others. The wise and confident acknowledge this help with gratitude."

ALFRED NORTH WHITEHEAD

"Gratitude is the appreciation of things that are not deserved, earned, or demanded—those wonderful things that we take for granted."

WILLIAM ARTHUR WARD

"Let us rise up and be thankful, for if we didn't learn a lot today, at least we learned a little, and if we didn't learn a little, at least we didn't get sick, and if we got sick, at least we didn't die; so, let us all be thankful."

BUDDHA

"Gratitude helps you to grow and expand; gratitude brings joy and laughter into your life and into the lives of all those around you."

EILEEN CADDY

If there is gratitude in your heart, then there will be tremendous sweetness in your eyes."

SRI CHINMOY

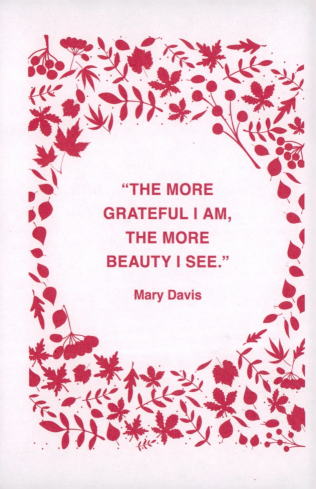

"The root of joy is gratefulness."

DAVID STEINDL-RAST

"Got no checkbooks, got no banks,
still I'd like to express my thanks.
I got the sun in the morning
and the moon at night."

IRVING BERLIN

> "What separates privilege from entitlement is gratitude."

BRENÉ BROWN

"Through the eyes of gratitude,
everything is a miracle."

MARY DAVIS

"Gratitude is the
sign of noble souls."

AESOP

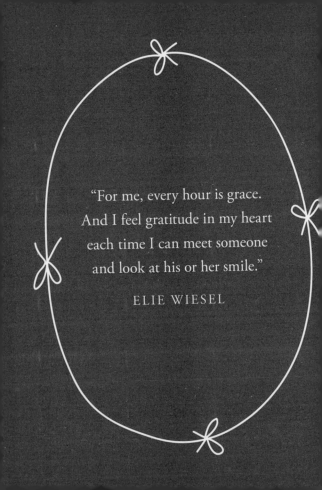

"For me, every hour is grace. And I feel gratitude in my heart each time I can meet someone and look at his or her smile."

ELIE WIESEL

"When I started counting my blessings, my whole life turned around."

WILLIE NELSON

"Strive to find things
to be thankful for,
and just look for the
good in who you are."

BETHANY HAMILTON

"If a fellow isn't thankful for what he's got, he isn't likely to be thankful for what he's going to get."

FRANK A. CLARK

"Be grateful in your own hearts. That suffices. Thanksgiving has wings, and flies to its right destination."

VICTOR HUGO

"The heart that gives thanks is a happy one, for we cannot feel thankful and unhappy at the same time."

DOUGLAS WOOD

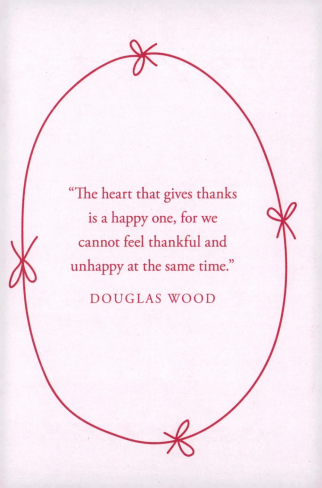

"I feel a very unusual sensation—if it is not indigestion, I think it must be gratitude."

BENJAMIN DISRAELI

"I have a lot to be thankful for.
I am healthy, happy
and I am loved."

REBA MCENTIRE

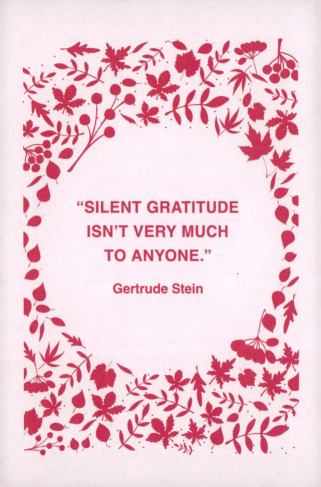

"We should certainly count our blessings, but we should also make our blessings count."

NEAL A. MAXWELL

"Two kinds of gratitude: The sudden kind we feel for what we take; the larger kind we feel for what we give."

EDWIN ARLINGTON ROBINSON

"If you fail to carry around with you a heart of gratitude for the love you've been so freely given, it is easy for you not to love others as you should."

PAUL DAVID TRIPP

"Who does not thank
for little will not
thank for much."

ESTONIAN
PROVERB

"Thanksgiving is a special virtue.
But ingratitude is
opposed to Thanksgiving.
Therefore ingratitude
is a special sin."

THOMAS AQUINAS

"We would worry less
if we praised more.
Thanksgiving is the enemy
of discontentand dissatisfaction."

HARRY A. IRONSIDE

"Not what we say
about our blessings,
but how we use them,
is the true measure
of our thanksgiving."

W. T. PURKISER

"Instead of thinking
'I will be happy when,'
try thinking
'I will be happy now'"

ANONYMOUS

"I can no other answer make,
but, thanks, And thanks,
and ever thanks."

WILLIAM SHAKESPEARE

"When gratitude becomes an essential foundation in our lives, miracles start to appear everywhere."

EMMANUEL DAGHER

"Living in a state of gratitude
is the gateway to grace."

ARIANNA HUFFINGTON

"The real gift of gratitude is that the more grateful you are, the more present you become."

ROBERT HOLDEN

In our pursuit of desire, we often overlook an invaluable virtue that has the power to transform lives: Gratitude.

Gratitude does not imply wearing perpetual rose-colored glasses, nor does it deter us from striving for more. It is simply the art of recognizing and appreciating the blessings, big or small, that grace our existence.

So, if you find yourself grappling with unfulfilled aspirations, embrace gratitude, acknowledge the goodness that surrounds you, and be thankful!

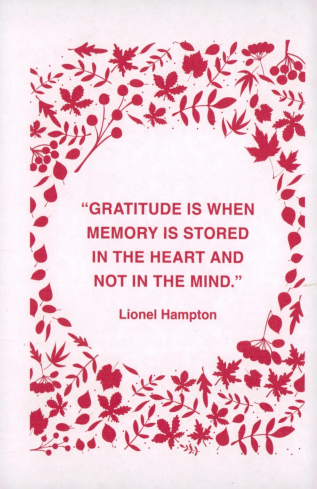

"When you arise in the morning give thanks for the food and for the joy of living. If you see no reason for giving thanks, the fault lies only in yourself."

TECUMSEH

"The roots of all goodness lie in the soil of appreciation for goodness."

14TH DALAI LAMA

"Gratitude can transform
common days
into thanksgivings,
turn routine jobs into joy,
and change ordinary
opportunities into blessings."

WILLIAM ARTHUR WARD

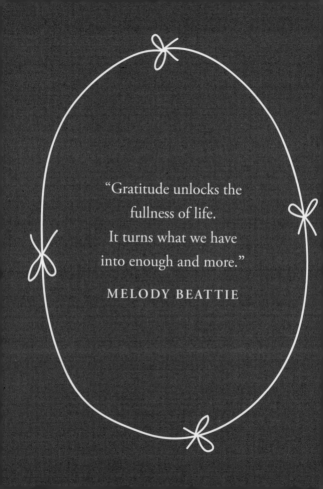

"Gratitude is not only the
greatest of virtues but
the parent of all others."

MARCUS TULLIUS CICERO

"As we express our gratitude,
we must never forget that
the highest appreciation
is not to utter words, but
to live by them."

JOHN F. KENNEDY

"The way to develop the best that is in a person is by appreciation and encouragement."

CHARLES SCHWAB

"Gratitude is the healthiest of all human emotions. The more you express gratitude for what you have, the more likely you will have even more to express gratitude for."

ZIG ZIGLAR

"When we focus
on our gratitude,
the tide of disappointment
goes out and the tide
of love rushes in."

KRISTIN ARMSTRONG

"Gratitude is the open
door to abundance."

ANONYMOUS

"Gratitude is an antidote to negative emotions, a neutralizer of envy, hostility, worry, and irritation. It is savoring; it is not taking things for granted; it is present-oriented."

SONJA LYUBOMIRSKY

"If you want to turn your life around, try thankfulness. It will change your life mightily."

GERALD GOOD

"Always have an attitude of gratitude."

STERLING K. BROWN

"We learned about gratitude and humility—that so many people had a hand in our success."

MICHELLE OBAMA

"I am happy
because I'm grateful.
I choose to be grateful.
That gratitude allows
me to be happy."

WILL ARNETT

"Gratitude also opens your eyes to the limitless potential of the universe, while dissatisfaction closes your eyes to it."

STEPHEN RICHARDS

"Some people grumble that roses have thorns; I am grateful that thorns have roses."

ALPHONSE KARR

"I think gratitude is a big thing.
It puts you in a place
where you're humble."

ANDRA DAY

"Gratitude is a quality
similar to electricity:
it must be produced and
discharged and used up
in order to exist at all."

WILLIAM FAULKNER

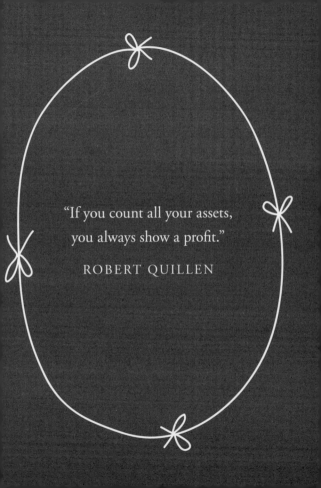

"If you count all your assets, you always show a profit."

ROBERT QUILLEN

"Gratitude is riches.
Complaint is poverty."

DORIS DAY

"To speak gratitude is courteous and pleasant, to enact gratitude is generous and noble, but to live gratitude is to touch Heaven."

JOHANNES A. GAERTNER

"In life, one has a choice to take one of two paths: to wait for some special day—or to celebrate each special day."

RASHEED OGUNLARU

"Gratitude is the sweetest thing in a seeker's life."

SRI CHINMOY

"Gratitude is the most
exquisite form of courtesy."

JACQUES MARITAIN

"Gratitude makes sense of our past, brings peace for today, and creates a vision for tomorrow."

MELODY BEATTIE

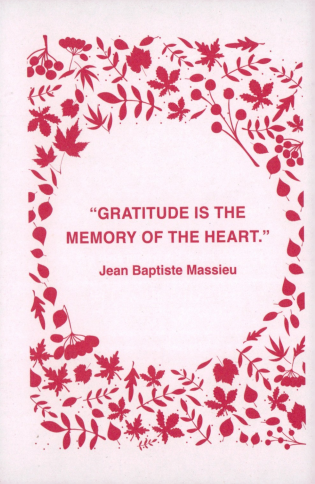

"Gratitude is a powerful catalyst for happiness. It's the spark that lights a fire of joy in your soul."

AMY COLLETTE

"'Thank you' is the best prayer that anyone could say."

ALICE WALKER

"Gratitude is a currency that we can mint for ourselves and spend without fear of bankruptcy."

FRED DE WITT VAN AMBURGH

"Everything we do should be a result of our gratitude for what God has done for us."

LAURYN HILL

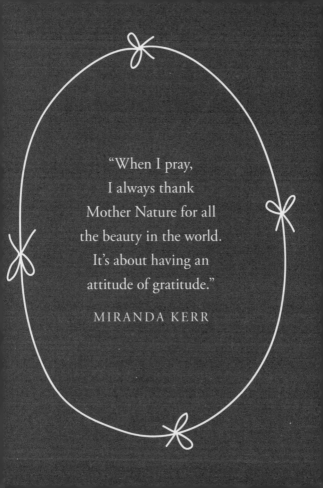

"When I pray, I always thank Mother Nature for all the beauty in the world. It's about having an attitude of gratitude."

MIRANDA KERR

"I awoke this morning with devout thanksgiving for my friends, the old and the new."

RALPH WALDO EMERSON

WHY IS GRATITUDE IMPORTANT?

★ Gratitude shifts the focus from what is lacking to what is present and by acknowledging and appreciating the blessings in our lives, we invite more positivity and abundance.

★ When we express gratitude towards others, we deepen the bond, build trust, and create a supportive environment.

★ Practicing gratitude improves our mental health. It can reduce stress, anxiety, and depression by promoting a sense of happiness and overall well-being.

★ It is a powerful tool to find silver linings and learn valuable lessons from adversity.

★ When we feel grateful, we are more likely to engage in acts of kindness.

"Appreciation is a wonderful thing. It makes what is excellent in others belong to us as well."

VOLTAIRE

"Happiness cannot travel to be owned, earned, worn or consumed. Happiness is the spiritual experience of living every minute with love, grace, and gratitude."

DENIS WAITLEY

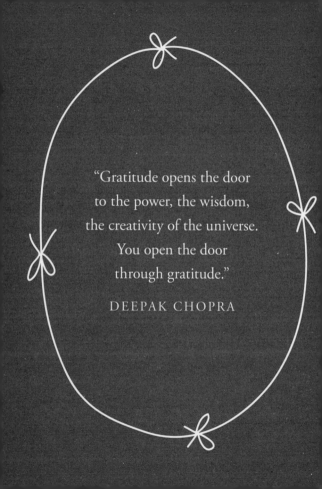

"Gratitude opens the door to the power, the wisdom, the creativity of the universe. You open the door through gratitude."

DEEPAK CHOPRA

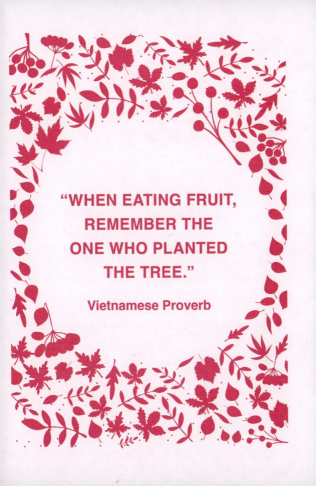

"Whatever we are waiting for—peace of mind, contentment, grace, the inner awareness of simple abundance—it will surely come to us, but only when we are ready to receive it with an open and grateful heart."

SARAH BAN BREATHNACH

"For my part, I am almost content
just now, and very thankful.
Gratitude is a divine emotion:
it fills the heart, but not to burst;
it warms it, but not to fever."

CHARLOTTE BRONTE

"No duty is more urgent than giving thanks."

JAMES ALLEN

"Gratitude is the music
of the heart, when its
chords are swept by
the breeze of kindness."

ANONYMOUS

"I would maintain that thanks are the highest form of thought, and that gratitude is happiness doubled by wonder."

G.K. CHESTERTON

"Enjoy the little things,
for one day you may look
back and realize they
were the big things."

ROBERT BRAULT

" 'Enough' is a feast."

BUDDHIST PROVERB

"He is a wise man who does not grieve for the things which he has not, but rejoices for those which he has."

EPICTETUS

"It's a funny thing about life, once you begin to take note of the things you are grateful for, you begin to lose sight of the things that you lack."

GERMANY KENT

"Gratitude is the music that dances within our souls, reminding us of the symphony of blessings that surround us every day."

ANONYMOUS

"In ordinary life, we hardly realize that we receive a great deal more than we give, and that it is only with gratitude that life becomes rich."

DIETRICH BONHOEFFER

"Piglet noticed that even though he had a Very Small Heart, it could hold a rather large amount of Gratitude."

A.A. MILNE

"Let us be grateful to the people who make us happy; they are the charming gardeners who make our souls blossom."

MARCEL PROUST

"Wear gratitude like a cloak, and it will feed every corner of your life."

RUMI

"True forgiveness
is when you can say,
'Thank you for
the experience.'"

OPRAH WINFREY

"Do not spoil what you have by desiring what you have not; remember that what you now have was once among the things you only hoped for."

EPICURUS

"Let gratitude be the pillow
upon which you kneel
to say your nightly prayer.
And let faith be the bridge
you build to overcome evil
and welcome good."

MAYA ANGELOU

"Cultivate the habit of being grateful for every good thing that comes to you, and to give thanks continuously. And because all things have contributed to your advancement, you should include all things in your gratitude."

RALPH WALDO EMERSON

"We must find time to stop
and thank the people who
make a difference in our lives."

JOHN F. KENNEDY

"When we express gratitude, we create ripples of love and kindness that reach far beyond our own understanding, touching the lives of others in ways we may never know."

ANONYMOUS

"If the only prayer you said was thank you, that would be enough."

MEISTER ECKHART

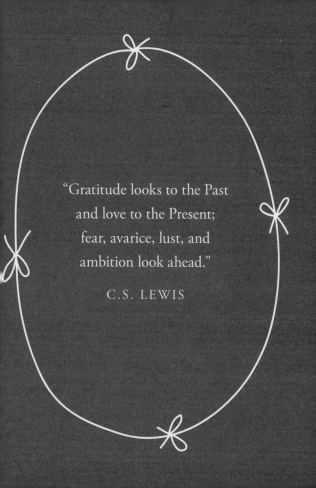

"Gratitude looks to the Past
and love to the Present;
fear, avarice, lust, and
ambition look ahead."

C.S. LEWIS

"Gratitude is the ability to experience life as a gift. It liberates us from the prison of self-preoccupation."

JOHN ORTBERG

"When it comes to life the critical thing is whether you take things for granted or take them with gratitude."

G.K. CHESTERTON

"The soul that gives thanks
can find comfort in everything;
the soul that complains can
find comfort in nothing."

HANNAH WHITALL SMITH

"O Lord that lends me life,
lend me a heart replete
with thankfulness."

WILLIAM SHAKESPEARE

"In the garden of life, gratitude is the sun that nurtures and brings beauty to every flower, no matter how small."

ANONYMOUS

"Reflect upon your present blessings,
of which every man has plenty;
not on your past misfortunes,
of which all men have some."

CHARLES DICKENS

"We can only be said to be alive in those moments when our hearts are conscious of our treasures."

THORNTON WILDER

"Gratitude and attitude
are not challenges;
they are choices."

ROBERT
BRAATHE

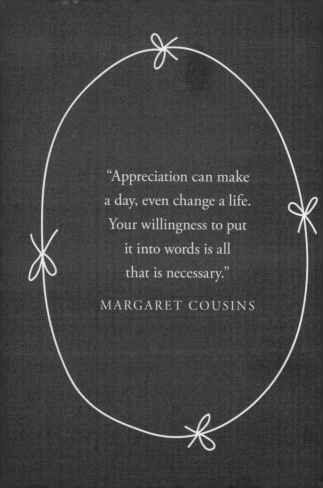

"Appreciation can make a day, even change a life. Your willingness to put it into words is all that is necessary."

MARGARET COUSINS

"Gratitude goes beyond the 'mine' and 'thine' and claims the truth that all of life is a pure gift."

HENRI J.M. NOUWEN

"Gratitude bestows reverence...
changing forever how
we experience life
and the world."

JOHN MILTON

"Thankfulness is the quickest path to joy."

JEFFERSON BETHKE

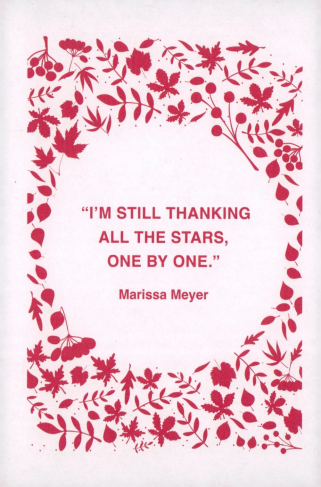

"Have gratitude for the things you're discarding. By giving gratitude, you're giving closure to the relationship with that object, and by doing so, it becomes a lot easier to let go."

MARIE KONDO

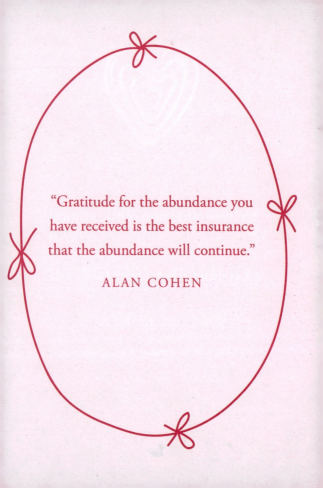

"Gratitude for the abundance you have received is the best insurance that the abundance will continue."

ALAN COHEN

"Sometimes we spend so much time and energy thinking about where we want to go that we don't notice where we happen to be."

DAN GUTMAN

"Don't pray when it rains if you don't pray when the sun shines."

LEROY SATCHEL PAIGE

"Learn to be thankful for what you already have, while you pursue all that you want."

JIM ROHN

"Gratitude paints little smiley faces on everything it touches."

RICHELLE E. GOODRICH